The

Grateful Living

Journal

A MORE MEANINGFUL
AND THRIVING WAY TO LIVE

By: _____

_____

Start date: _____ / _____ / _____

The Grateful Living Journal: A More Meaningful and Thriving Way to Live by Kristy Nelson
Paperback
Categories: Self-Help
Cover and Interior Design: Luz Linea Studios
Editor: Lisa Parry

ISBN: 979-8-218-18687-6
First Edition

The intent of this publication is only to offer information of a general nature to help in your quest for emotional and spiritual well-being. The ideas and techniques contained in the book are not intended as a substitute for advice from a physician. In the event you use any of the information in this book for yourself, the author and publisher assume no responsibility for your actions.

Introduction

Welcome to **The Grateful Living** journey.
I am so happy and grateful we are here together.

I have learned the secrets to thriving, the secrets to happiness and joy.

They are:
1. We must create space for and take care of ourselves.
2. We must stay in the present moment and with the people around us (mindfulness).
3. We must be grateful, be expectant of good outcomes, and start looking for the good in the world.

Changes, transitions, and even wilderness seasons can be a bit challenging to walk through. We must remember, though, that with a grateful heart and an intention to be curious, these seasons can add great value that leads to unlimited possibilities for living in a more meaningful, mindful, and thriving way.

Through this journal, you, too, will uncover the secrets.

My Story

This **Grateful Living** journey started for me when I walked through many transitional seasons. The one that impacted me most was going from corporate life to farm wife. After twelve years in the corporate world, my husband and I decided it was time to focus more on our family, so I packed up and took what I learned in the corporate world home with me.

Now this may sound like a simple transition, but it has taken me ten years to fully accept my role as not only a wife to a farmer but also my identity as a mother, daughter, daughter-in-law, and entrepreneur. All the while, in joining my husband with his passions to feed the world, I began to feel a deep connection with farming as I have been slowly discovering my authentic self. From the outside looking in, it looked all good, but on the inside, there was war and chaos raging as I trudged through these transitional and wilderness seasons.

I had no peace.

I became exhausted by comparing myself to others and trying to identify and grow comfortable with my new role. I also was trying to be who everyone else wanted me to be until some unexpected people at unexpected times showed up in my life. I am truly grateful for my mentors, coaches, counselors, and friends who have made a significant positive impact on my life. They have shared many tools and practices that have shaped and helped me manage my stress and anxiety. In time, they guided me to my authentic self.

Grateful Living is more than two words working together. It is a lifestyle, a state of mind, and an attitude of being that will help shift one's focus from negative mental habits to a more positive, joyful state of being. When we are grateful and take the time to express our thankfulness, we ultimately realize how truly blessed we are. Sometimes, Grateful Living can be challenging... especially when life presents us with challenges. We tend to revert to our natural state, our reactive state, and our old ways of thinking. It's through the practices in this journal that we can help shift our focus and mindset. It's in this state of contentment that will have a lasting impact to help you make that shift. It's the feeling of joy, love, happiness, and genuine warmth that will shift our minds and hearts into a more peaceful and open state. This feeling of gratitude helps to recenter and ground ourselves in the knowledge that God is in all things and in control of all things.

I am looking forward to walking you through what I learned, and my hope is you too will find peace, love, joy, and the unlimited possibilities to live in a more meaningful, mindful, and thriving way. So welcome to our Grateful Living.

With a grateful heart,   Kristy Nelson

Grateful Living Journey

The definition of gratitude is the quality of being thankful; readiness to show appreciation for and to return kindness. Gratefulness is defined as feeling or showing an appreciation of kindness; thankful. So, in essence, gratefulness is the **feeling** generated from our gratitude. In positive psychology research, gratitude has a strong correlation with greater happiness. When we focus on what is good, savor good experiences, and pause to notice and appreciate those good things, our mind shifts into a more positive state. This shift will build strong relationships with others and ourselves. It will also help us in becoming a more resilient person with better overall health.

The tools I have accumulated are what I practice every day to help organize my thoughts, bring awareness to the present moment, and help me prioritize what is important to my wellbeing.

Through this guided Grateful Living Journal, we will explore ways of living life in a more meaningful and mindful way. Being present in the moment instead of living in the past or the future has been shown to help reduce stress and anxiety. Gratitude encourages us to notice the little things. Gratitude increases dopamine levels in our brains, and it stimulates the hypothalamus which keeps our entire body system in check. Gratitude has been shown to improve physical health, sleep, reduces inflammation, and helps us feel just plain good.

Once we begin this practice of gratitude, our brains will automatically seek out good things. When we focus on good things, we are able to focus with ease and stop wasting energy on worry, fear or doubt.

Grateful Living Journal Summary

Section 1 - I am so grateful and thankful for:

Write out three to five or ten things—people, places, possessions, etc.—you truly appreciate. Really feel the emotion of each appreciation and savor them. Use your five senses. As you feel the appreciation, your heart will begin to expand and feel relaxed. It's in this state of appreciation we begin to open up our hearts and begin to let the day flow with ease.

Section 2 - Goals

Today's Priority Goals (Goals that you must do today):

Write out three priority goals you know you need to accomplish today. By writing out what we must do, we ease our minds into a relaxed state. There is something about putting it down on paper that helps tell the mind "Ok, I got it, I can do this, I accept the challenge." This practice creates space for our minds to ease up, creates clarity and focus, and helps us to accept our circumstances as they are.

Today's Fun Goals (Goals that bring you joy):

Write out three fun goals that you can do for you. These should be goals that make you happy and give you a sense of purpose. These types of goals create space for self-care, being your authentic self, and curiosity. The fun goals will help us reset when life happens and we need to refocus to get back on track. Examples may be going for a walk, tinkering in the garage, gardening, reading a book, or playing games.

Section 3 - Journal Entry

Use this free space to write out your thoughts or anything else that seems to need to move from your mind to the page. You may write out a prayer or use this space to reflect on your day.

The Grateful Living Journal is a journal created to support you and can be enjoyed any time of the day that works best. It is a journal that is about you and helping you find peace and joy so you can live in a more meaningful, mindful, and thriving way. On this journey, there will be days that don't go as planned so you do not find time to journal. That is OK. Give yourself permission to miss a day. Grant yourself grace. If at the end of the day you find that you only have time to journal one section, that is awesome. Celebrate you!

Every day is a new start. Why not start with a grateful heart?

25 Fun Activities List

What brings you joy? What activities do you like to do just for you, for fun? In this space, write down 25 things you enjoy doing or would like to do some time.

Each day we are given an opportunity to live the Best Day Ever, and it's through these fun activities we enjoy participating in that bring happiness and joy. Living your Best Day Ever is about being grateful, taking care of yourself, being your authentic self, and being curious about the world around you. Through these fun activities, you help reset yourself when you get off track. Plus, your heart will thank you for keeping you a priority.

Living your Best Day Ever brings you back to finding the rhythm of your authentic self.

So go for it. Take a few moments to write out some fun activities you enjoy. You will use this list on the days you may forget what fun looks like when you start using the journal. You can start off with a few, but, remember you can always add to the list because each day is meant to be enjoyed.

I am so grateful and thankful for:

(Note what you truly appreciate. Really feel the emotion of appreciation. Utilize your five senses.)

1.

2.

3.

4.

5.

6.

7.

8.

9.

10.

Today's Priority Goals:
(Goals you must reach today.)

1. _____

2. _____

3. _____

Fun Goals:
(Goals that bring you joy.)

1. _____

2. _____

3. _____

Journal Entry/Notes:

(Use this space to expand on your thoughts.)

_____

_____

_____

_____

_____

_____

_____

_____

_____

_____

_____

_____

_____

_____

_____

Date ___ / ___ / ___

I am so grateful and thankful for:

(Note what you truly appreciate. Really feel the emotion of appreciation. Utilize your five senses.)

1.

2.

3.

4.

5.

6.

7.

8.

9.

10.

When we focus on our gratitude, the tide of disappointment goes out and the tide of love rushes in.

Kristin Armstrong

Today's Priority Goals:
(Goals you must reach today.)

1. _____
2. _____
3. _____

Fun Goals:
(Goals that bring you joy.)

1. _____
2. _____
3. _____

Journal Entry/Notes:

(Use this space to expand on your thoughts.)

Date / /

$\mathcal{I}$ am so grateful and thankful for:

(Note what you truly appreciate. Really feel the emotion of appreciation. Utilize your five senses.)

1.

2.

3.

4.

5.

6.

7.

8.

9.

10.

Today's Priority Goals:
(Goals you must reach today.)

1. _____
2. _____
3. _____

Fun Goals:
(Goals that bring you joy.)

1. _____
2. _____
3. _____

Journal Entry/Notes:

(Use this space to expand on your thoughts.)

_____
_____
_____
_____
_____
_____
_____
_____
_____
_____
_____
_____
_____
_____
_____

Date / /

I am so grateful and thankful for:

(Note what you truly appreciate. Really feel the emotion of appreciation. Utilize your five senses.)

1.

2.

3.

4.

5.

6.

7.

8.

9.

10.

Today's Priority Goals:
(Goals you must reach today.)

1.
2.
3.

Fun Goals:
(Goals that bring you joy.)

1.
2.
3.

Journal Entry/Notes:

(Use this space to expand on your thoughts.)

Date / /

I am so grateful and thankful for:

(Note what you truly appreciate. Really feel the emotion of appreciation. Utilize your five senses.)

1.

2.

3.

4.

5.

6.

7.

8.

9.

10.

Today's Priority Goals:
(Goals you must reach today.)

1. _____
2. _____
3. _____

Fun Goals:
(Goals that bring you joy.)

1. _____
2. _____
3. _____

Journal Entry/Notes:

(Use this space to expand on your thoughts.)

I am so grateful and thankful for:

(Note what you truly appreciate. Really feel the emotion of appreciation. Utilize your five senses.)

1.

2.

3.

4.

5.

6.

7.

8.

9.

10.

Change your thoughts and you change your world.

Norman Vincent Peale

Today's Priority Goals:
(Goals you must reach today.)

1.
2.
3.

Fun Goals:
(Goals that bring you joy.)

1.
2.
3.

Journal Entry/Notes:

(Use this space to expand on your thoughts.)

I am so grateful and thankful for:

(Note what you truly appreciate. Really feel the emotion of appreciation. Utilize your five senses.)

1.

2.

3.

4.

5.

6.

7.

8.

9.

10.

Today's Priority Goals:
(Goals you must reach today.)

1.

2.

3.

Fun Goals:
(Goals that bring you joy.)

1.

2.

3.

Journal Entry/Notes:

(Use this space to expand on your thoughts.)

Date ___ / ___ / ___

I am so grateful and thankful for:

(Note what you truly appreciate. Really feel the emotion of appreciation. Utilize your five senses.)

1. _____

2. _____

3. _____

4. _____

5. _____

6. _____

7. _____

8. _____

9. _____

10. _____

Today's Priority Goals:
(Goals you must reach today.)

1. _____
2. _____
3. _____

Fun Goals:
(Goals that bring you joy.)

1. _____
2. _____
3. _____

Journal Entry/Notes:

(Use this space to expand on your thoughts.)

_____
_____
_____
_____
_____
_____
_____
_____
_____
_____
_____
_____
_____
_____

I am so grateful and thankful for:

(Note what you truly appreciate. Really feel the emotion of appreciation. Utilize your five senses.)

1.

2.

3.

4.

5.

6.

7.

8.

9.

10.

Today's Priority Goals:
(Goals you must reach today.)

1.

2.

3.

Fun Goals:
(Goals that bring you joy.)

1.

2.

3.

Journal Entry/Notes:

(Use this space to expand on your thoughts.)

Date _____ / ___ / ___

I am so grateful and thankful for:

(Note what you truly appreciate. Really feel the emotion of appreciation. Utilize your five senses.)

1. _____

2. _____

3. _____

4. _____

5. _____

6. _____

7. _____

8. _____

9. _____

10. _____

The root of joy is gratefulness. It is not joy that makes us grateful; it is gratitude that makes us joyful.

Brother David Steindl-Rast

Today's Priority Goals:
(Goals you must reach today.)

1. _____

2. _____

3. _____

Fun Goals:
(Goals that bring you joy.)

1. _____

2. _____

3. _____

Journal Entry/Notes:

(Use this space to expand on your thoughts.)

I am so grateful and thankful for:

(Note what you truly appreciate. Really feel the emotion of appreciation. Utilize your five senses.)

1.

2.

3.

4.

5.

6.

7.

8.

9.

10.

Today's Priority Goals:
(Goals you must reach today.)

1.

2.

3.

Fun Goals:
(Goals that bring you joy.)

1.

2.

3.

Journal Entry/Notes:

(Use this space to expand on your thoughts.)

$\mathcal{I}$ am so grateful and thankful for:

(Note what you truly appreciate. Really feel the emotion of appreciation. Utilize your five senses.)

1.

2.

3.

4.

5.

6.

7.

8.

9.

10.

Today's Priority Goals:
(Goals you must reach today.)

1. _____

2. _____

3. _____

Fun Goals:
(Goals that bring you joy.)

1. _____

2. _____

3. _____

Journal Entry/Notes:

(Use this space to expand on your thoughts.)

I am so grateful and thankful for:

(Note what you truly appreciate. Really feel the emotion of appreciation. Utilize your five senses.)

1.

2.

3.

4.

5.

6.

7.

8.

9.

10.

Today's Priority Goals:
(Goals you must reach today.)

1. _____

2. _____

3. _____

Fun Goals:
(Goals that bring you joy.)

1. _____

2. _____

3. _____

Journal Entry/Notes:

(Use this space to expand on your thoughts.)

_____

_____

_____

_____

_____

_____

_____

_____

_____

_____

_____

_____

_____

_____

Date ___/___/___

$\mathcal{I}$ am so grateful and thankful for:
(Note what you truly appreciate. Really feel the emotion of appreciation. Utilize your five senses.)

1.

2.

3.

4.

5.

6.

7.

8.

9.

10.

Taking good care of YOU, means the people in your life will receive the best of you, rather than what's left of you.

Carl Bryan

Today's Priority Goals:
(Goals you must reach today.)

1. _____

2. _____

3. _____

Fun Goals:
(Goals that bring you joy.)

1. _____

2. _____

3. _____

Journal Entry/Notes:

(Use this space to expand on your thoughts.)

I am so grateful and thankful for:

(Note what you truly appreciate. Really feel the emotion of appreciation. Utilize your five senses.)

1.

2.

3.

4.

5.

6.

7.

8.

9.

10.

Today's Priority Goals:
(Goals you must reach today.)

1. _____

2. _____

3. _____

Fun Goals:
(Goals that bring you joy.)

1. _____

2. _____

3. _____

Journal Entry/Notes:

(Use this space to expand on your thoughts.)

_____

_____

_____

_____

_____

_____

_____

_____

_____

_____

_____

_____

_____

Date / /

I am so grateful and thankful for:

(Note what you truly appreciate. Really feel the emotion of appreciation. Utilize your five senses.)

1.
2.
3.
4.
5.
6.
7.
8.
9.
10.

Today's Priority Goals:
(Goals you must reach today.)

1.
2.
3.

Fun Goals:
(Goals that bring you joy.)

1.
2.
3.

Journal Entry/Notes:
(Use this space to expand on your thoughts.)

Date __/__/__

I am so grateful and thankful for:

(Note what you truly appreciate. Really feel the emotion of appreciation. Utilize your five senses.)

1. _____

2. _____

3. _____

4. _____

5. _____

6. _____

7. _____

8. _____

9. _____

10. _____

Today's Priority Goals:
(Goals you must reach today.)

1. _____

2. _____

3. _____

Fun Goals:
(Goals that bring you joy.)

1. _____

2. _____

3. _____

Journal Entry/Notes:

(Use this space to expand on your thoughts.)

_____

_____

_____

_____

_____

_____

_____

_____

_____

_____

_____

_____

_____

Date / /

I am so grateful and thankful for:

(Note what you truly appreciate. Really feel the emotion of appreciation. Utilize your five senses.)

1.

2.

3.

4.

5.

6.

7.

8.

9.

10.

You will discover that you have two hands. One is for helping yourself and the other is for helping others.

Audrey Hepburn

Today's Priority Goals:
(Goals you must reach today.)

1. _____

2. _____

3. _____

Fun Goals:
(Goals that bring you joy.)

1. _____

2. _____

3. _____

Journal Entry/Notes:

(Use this space to expand on your thoughts.)

_____

_____

_____

_____

_____

_____

_____

_____

_____

_____

_____

_____

_____

_____

_____

_____

Date / /

$\mathcal{I}$ am so grateful and thankful for:

(Note what you truly appreciate. Really feel the emotion of appreciation. Utilize your five senses.)

1.

2.

3.

4.

5.

6.

7.

8.

9.

10.

Today's Priority Goals:
(Goals you must reach today.)

1. _____

2. _____

3. _____

Fun Goals:
(Goals that bring you joy.)

1. _____

2. _____

3. _____

Journal Entry/Notes:

(Use this space to expand on your thoughts.)

_____

_____

_____

_____

_____

_____

_____

_____

_____

_____

_____

_____

_____

_____

_____

I am so grateful and thankful for:

(Note what you truly appreciate. Really feel the emotion of appreciation. Utilize your five senses.)

1.

2.

3.

4.

5.

6.

7.

8.

9.

10.

Today's Priority Goals:
(Goals you must reach today.)

1. _____

2. _____

3. _____

Fun Goals:
(Goals that bring you joy.)

1. _____

2. _____

3. _____

Journal Entry/Notes:

(Use this space to expand on your thoughts.)

_____

_____

_____

_____

_____

_____

_____

_____

_____

_____

_____

_____

I am so grateful and thankful for:

(Note what you truly appreciate. Really feel the emotion of appreciation. Utilize your five senses.)

1.

2.

3.

4.

5.

6.

7.

8.

9.

10.

Today's Priority Goals:
(Goals you must reach today.)

1. _____

2. _____

3. _____

Fun Goals:
(Goals that bring you joy.)

1. _____

2. _____

3. _____

Journal Entry/Notes:

(Use this space to expand on your thoughts.)

_____

_____

_____

_____

_____

_____

_____

_____

_____

_____

_____

_____

_____

_____

Date / /

$\mathcal{I}$ am so grateful and thankful for:

(Note what you truly appreciate. Really feel the emotion of appreciation. Utilize your five senses.)

1.

2.

3.

4.

5.

6.

7.

8.

9.

10.

The best and most beautiful things in the world cannot be seen or even touched-they must be felt with the heart.

Helen Keller

Today's Priority Goals:
(Goals you must reach today.)

1. _____

2. _____

3. _____
_____

Fun Goals:
(Goals that bring you joy.)

1. _____

2. _____

3. _____
_____

Journal Entry/Notes:

(Use this space to expand on your thoughts.)

_____
_____
_____
_____
_____
_____
_____
_____
_____
_____
_____
_____
_____
_____
_____
_____

Date ___/___/___

$\mathcal{I}$ am so grateful and thankful for:

(Note what you truly appreciate. Really feel the emotion of appreciation. Utilize your five senses.)

1.

2.

3.

4.

5.

6.

7.

8.

9.

10.

Today's Priority Goals:
(Goals you must reach today.)

1. _____

2. _____

3. _____

Fun Goals:
(Goals that bring you joy.)

1. _____

2. _____

3. _____

Journal Entry/Notes:

(Use this space to expand on your thoughts.)

Date / /

$\mathcal{I}$ am so grateful and thankful for:

(Note what you truly appreciate. Really feel the emotion of appreciation. Utilize your five senses.)

1.

2.

3.

4.

5.

6.

7.

8.

9.

10.

Today's Priority Goals:
(Goals you must reach today.)

1. _____
2. _____
3. _____

Fun Goals:
(Goals that bring you joy.)

1. _____
2. _____
3. _____

Journal Entry/Notes:

(Use this space to expand on your thoughts.)

_____
_____
_____
_____
_____
_____
_____
_____
_____
_____
_____
_____
_____
_____

Date ___ / ___ / ___

I am so grateful and thankful for:

(Note what you truly appreciate. Really feel the emotion of appreciation. Utilize your five senses.)

1.

2.

3.

4.

5.

6.

7.

8.

9.

10.

Today's Priority Goals:
(Goals you must reach today.)

1.

2.

3.

Fun Goals:
(Goals that bring you joy.)

1.

2.

3.

Journal Entry/Notes:

(Use this space to expand on your thoughts.)

I am so grateful and thankful for:

(Note what you truly appreciate. Really feel the emotion of appreciation. Utilize your five senses.)

1.

2.

3.

4.

5.

6.

7.

8.

9.

10.

Promise me you'll always remember: you're braver than you believe, stronger than you seem, and smarter than you think.

Winnie-the-Pooh

Today's Priority Goals:
(Goals you must reach today.)

1. _____

2. _____

3. _____

Fun Goals:
(Goals that bring you joy.)

1. _____

2. _____

3. _____

Journal Entry/Notes:

(Use this space to expand on your thoughts.)

_____

_____

_____

_____

_____

_____

_____

_____

_____

_____

_____

_____

_____

_____

_____

_____

I am so grateful and thankful for:

(Note what you truly appreciate. Really feel the emotion of appreciation. Utilize your five senses.)

1.

2.

3.

4.

5.

6.

7.

8.

9.

10.

Today's Priority Goals:
(Goals you must reach today.)

1. _____

2. _____

3. _____

Fun Goals:
(Goals that bring you joy.)

1. _____

2. _____

3. _____

Journal Entry/Notes:

(Use this space to expand on your thoughts.)

_____

_____

_____

_____

_____

_____

_____

_____

_____

_____

_____

_____

_____

I am so grateful and thankful for:

(Note what you truly appreciate. Really feel the emotion of appreciation. Utilize your five senses.)

1.

2.

3.

4.

5.

6.

7.

8.

9.

10.

Today's Priority Goals:
(Goals you must reach today.)

1. _____
2. _____
3. _____

Fun Goals:
(Goals that bring you joy.)

1. _____
2. _____
3. _____

Journal Entry/Notes:

(Use this space to expand on your thoughts.)

Date / /

I am so grateful and thankful for:

(Note what you truly appreciate. Really feel the emotion of appreciation. Utilize your five senses.)

1.

2.

3.

4.

5.

6.

7.

8.

9.

10.

Today's Priority Goals:
(Goals you must reach today.)

1.
2.
3.

Fun Goals:
(Goals that bring you joy.)

1.
2.
3.

Journal Entry/Notes:

(Use this space to expand on your thoughts.)

I am so grateful and thankful for:

(Note what you truly appreciate. Really feel the emotion of appreciation. Utilize your five senses.)

1.

2.

3.

4.

5.

6.

7.

8.

9.

10.

You can't go back and change the beginning, but you can start where you are and change the ending.

C S Lewis

Today's Priority Goals:
(Goals you must reach today.)

1. _____
2. _____
3. _____

Fun Goals:
(Goals that bring you joy.)

1. _____
2. _____
3. _____

Journal Entry/Notes:

(Use this space to expand on your thoughts.)

I am so grateful and thankful for:

(Note what you truly appreciate. Really feel the emotion of appreciation. Utilize your five senses.)

1.

2.

3.

4.

5.

6.

7.

8.

9.

10.

Today's Priority Goals:
(Goals you must reach today.)

1. _____

2. _____

3. _____

Fun Goals:
(Goals that bring you joy.)

1. _____

2. _____

3. _____

Journal Entry/Notes:

(Use this space to expand on your thoughts.)

_____

_____

_____

_____

_____

_____

_____

_____

_____

_____

_____

_____

_____

_____

_____

Date   /   /

$\mathscr{I}$ am so grateful and thankful for:

(Note what you truly appreciate. Really feel the emotion of appreciation.
Utilize your five senses.)

1.

2.

3.

4.

5.

6.

7.

8.

9.

10.

Today's Priority Goals:
(Goals you must reach today.)

1. _____
2. _____
3. _____

Fun Goals:
(Goals that bring you joy.)

1. _____
2. _____
3. _____

Journal Entry/Notes:

(Use this space to expand on your thoughts.)

I am so grateful and thankful for:

(Note what you truly appreciate. Really feel the emotion of appreciation. Utilize your five senses.)

1.

2.

3.

4.

5.

6.

7.

8.

9.

10.

Today's Priority Goals:
(Goals you must reach today.)

1. _____
2. _____
3. _____

Fun Goals:
(Goals that bring you joy.)

1. _____
2. _____
3. _____

Journal Entry/Notes:

(Use this space to expand on your thoughts.)

Date / /

$\mathcal{I}$ am so grateful and thankful for:

(Note what you truly appreciate. Really feel the emotion of appreciation. Utilize your five senses.)

1.

2.

3.

4.

5.

6.

7.

8.

9.

10.

Gratitude turns what we have into enough, and more. It turns denial into acceptance, chaos into order, confusion into clarity... it makes sense of our past, brings peace for today, and creates a vision for tomorrow.

Melody Beattie

Today's Priority Goals:
(Goals you must reach today.)

1.

2.

3.

Fun Goals:
(Goals that bring you joy.)

1.

2.

3.

Journal Entry/Notes:

(Use this space to expand on your thoughts.)

Date / /

I am so grateful and thankful for:

(Note what you truly appreciate. Really feel the emotion of appreciation. Utilize your five senses.)

1.

2.

3.

4.

5.

6.

7.

8.

9.

10.

Today's Priority Goals:
(Goals you must reach today.)

1.
2.
3.

Fun Goals:
(Goals that bring you joy.)

1.
2.
3.

Journal Entry/Notes:

(Use this space to expand on your thoughts.)

Date / /

I am so grateful and thankful for:

(Note what you truly appreciate. Really feel the emotion of appreciation. Utilize your five senses.)

1.

2.

3.

4.

5.

6.

7.

8.

9.

10.

Today's Priority Goals:
(Goals you must reach today.)

1. _____

2. _____

3. _____

Fun Goals:
(Goals that bring you joy.)

1. _____

2. _____

3. _____

Journal Entry/Notes:

(Use this space to expand on your thoughts.)

_____

_____

_____

_____

_____

_____

_____

_____

_____

_____

_____

_____

_____

_____

_____

I am so grateful and thankful for:

(Note what you truly appreciate. Really feel the emotion of appreciation. Utilize your five senses.)

1.

2.

3.

4.

5.

6.

7.

8.

9.

10.

Today's Priority Goals:
(Goals you must reach today.)

1.

2.

3.

Fun Goals:
(Goals that bring you joy.)

1.

2.

3.

Journal Entry/Notes:

(Use this space to expand on your thoughts.)

I am so grateful and thankful for:

(Note what you truly appreciate. Really feel the emotion of appreciation. Utilize your five senses.)

1.

2.

3.

4.

5.

6.

7.

8.

9.

10.

Gratitude is a powerful catalyst for happiness. It's the spark that lights a fire of joy in your soul.

Amy Collette

Today's Priority Goals:
(Goals you must reach today.)

1. _____
2. _____
3. _____

Fun Goals:
(Goals that bring you joy.)

1. _____
2. _____
3. _____

Journal Entry/Notes:
(Use this space to expand on your thoughts.)

_____
_____
_____
_____
_____
_____
_____
_____
_____
_____
_____
_____
_____
_____

Date ___ / ___ / ___

I am so grateful and thankful for:

(Note what you truly appreciate. Really feel the emotion of appreciation. Utilize your five senses.)

1. _____

2. _____

3. _____

4. _____

5. _____

6. _____

7. _____

8. _____

9. _____

10. _____

Today's Priority Goals:
(Goals you must reach today.)

1. _____
2. _____
3. _____

Fun Goals:
(Goals that bring you joy.)

1. _____
2. _____
3. _____

Journal Entry/Notes:

(Use this space to expand on your thoughts.)

_____
_____
_____
_____
_____
_____
_____
_____
_____
_____
_____
_____
_____
_____

Date / /

I am so grateful and thankful for:

(Note what you truly appreciate. Really feel the emotion of appreciation. Utilize your five senses.)

1.

2.

3.

4.

5.

6.

7.

8.

9.

10.

Today's Priority Goals:
(Goals you must reach today.)

1. _____

2. _____

3. _____

Fun Goals:
(Goals that bring you joy.)

1. _____

2. _____

3. _____

Journal Entry/Notes:

(Use this space to expand on your thoughts.)

_____

_____

_____

_____

_____

_____

_____

_____

_____

_____

_____

_____

_____

_____

_____

_____

_____

I am so grateful and thankful for:

(Note what you truly appreciate. Really feel the emotion of appreciation. Utilize your five senses.)

1.

2.

3.

4.

5.

6.

7.

8.

9.

10.

Today's Priority Goals:
(Goals you must reach today.)

1.

2.

3.

Fun Goals:
(Goals that bring you joy.)

1.

2.

3.

Journal Entry/Notes:

(Use this space to expand on your thoughts.)

I am so grateful and thankful for:

(Note what you truly appreciate. Really feel the emotion of appreciation. Utilize your five senses.)

1.

2.

3.

4.

5.

6.

7.

8.

9.

10.

It takes a lot of courage to have an attitude of gratitude during the dark times. But once you have it, it empowers you.

Joshua Tongol

Today's Priority Goals:
(Goals you must reach today.)

1.

2.

3.

Fun Goals:
(Goals that bring you joy.)

1.

2.

3.

Journal Entry/Notes:

(Use this space to expand on your thoughts.)

I am so grateful and thankful for:

(Note what you truly appreciate. Really feel the emotion of appreciation. Utilize your five senses.)

1.

2.

3.

4.

5.

6.

7.

8.

9.

10.

Today's Priority Goals:
(Goals you must reach today.)

1.

2.

3.

Fun Goals:
(Goals that bring you joy.)

1.

2.

3.

Journal Entry/Notes:

(Use this space to expand on your thoughts.)

Date / /

I am so grateful and thankful for:

(Note what you truly appreciate. Really feel the emotion of appreciation. Utilize your five senses.)

1.

2.

3.

4.

5.

6.

7.

8.

9.

10.

Today's Priority Goals:
(Goals you must reach today.)

1. _____
2. _____
3. _____

Fun Goals:
(Goals that bring you joy.)

1. _____
2. _____
3. _____

Journal Entry/Notes:

(Use this space to expand on your thoughts.)

_____
_____
_____
_____
_____
_____
_____
_____
_____
_____
_____
_____
_____

I am so grateful and thankful for:

(Note what you truly appreciate. Really feel the emotion of appreciation. Utilize your five senses.)

1.

2.

3.

4.

5.

6.

7.

8.

9.

10.

Today's Priority Goals:
(Goals you must reach today.)

1. _____

2. _____

3. _____

Fun Goals:
(Goals that bring you joy.)

1. _____

2. _____

3. _____

Journal Entry/Notes:

(Use this space to expand on your thoughts.)

_____

_____

_____

_____

_____

_____

_____

_____

_____

_____

_____

_____

_____

_____

Date ____ / ____ / ____

I am so grateful and thankful for:

(Note what you truly appreciate. Really feel the emotion of appreciation. Utilize your five senses.)

1.

2.

3.

4.

5.

6.

7.

8.

9.

10.

The thankful heart opens our eyes to a multitude of blessings that continually surround us.

James E. Faust

Today's Priority Goals:
(Goals you must reach today.)

1. _____

2. _____

3. _____

Fun Goals:
(Goals that bring you joy.)

1. _____

2. _____

3. _____

Journal Entry/Notes:

(Use this space to expand on your thoughts.)

_____

_____

_____

_____

_____

_____

_____

_____

_____

_____

_____

_____

_____

_____

_____

_____

_____

I am so grateful and thankful for:

(Note what you truly appreciate. Really feel the emotion of appreciation. Utilize your five senses.)

1.

2.

3.

4.

5.

6.

7.

8.

9.

10.

Today's Priority Goals:
(Goals you must reach today.)

1. _____
2. _____
3. _____

Fun Goals:
(Goals that bring you joy.)

1. _____
2. _____
3. _____

Journal Entry/Notes:

(Use this space to expand on your thoughts.)

Date ___ / ___ / ___

I am so grateful and thankful for:

(Note what you truly appreciate. Really feel the emotion of appreciation. Utilize your five senses.)

1.

2.

3.

4.

5.

6.

7.

8.

9.

10.

Today's Priority Goals:
(Goals you must reach today.)

1.

2.

3.

Fun Goals:
(Goals that bring you joy.)

1.

2.

3.

Journal Entry/Notes:

(Use this space to expand on your thoughts.)

Date ___/___/___

I am so grateful and thankful for:

(Note what you truly appreciate. Really feel the emotion of appreciation. Utilize your five senses.)

1. _____

2. _____

3. _____

4. _____

5. _____

6. _____

7. _____

8. _____

9. _____

10. _____

Today's Priority Goals:
(Goals you must reach today.)

1. _____

2. _____

3. _____

Fun Goals:
(Goals that bring you joy.)

1. _____

2. _____

3. _____

Journal Entry/Notes:

(Use this space to expand on your thoughts.)

_____
_____
_____
_____
_____
_____
_____
_____
_____
_____
_____
_____
_____

Date ___ / ___ / ___

I am so grateful and thankful for:

(Note what you truly appreciate. Really feel the emotion of appreciation. Utilize your five senses.)

1. _____

2. _____

3. _____

4. _____

5. _____

6. _____

7. _____

8. _____

9. _____

10. _____

As we express our gratitude, we must never forget that the highest appreciation is not to utter words but to live by them.

John F. Kennedy

Today's Priority Goals:
(Goals you must reach today.)

1. _____
2. _____
3. _____

Fun Goals:
(Goals that bring you joy.)

1. _____
2. _____
3. _____

Journal Entry/Notes:

(Use this space to expand on your thoughts.)

Date / /

ℐ am so grateful and thankful for:

(Note what you truly appreciate. Really feel the emotion of appreciation. Utilize your five senses.)

1.

2.

3.

4.

5.

6.

7.

8.

9.

10.

Today's Priority Goals:
(Goals you must reach today.)

1. _____

2. _____

3. _____

Fun Goals:
(Goals that bring you joy.)

1. _____

2. _____

3. _____

Journal Entry/Notes:

(Use this space to expand on your thoughts.)

Date ___ / ___ / ___

$\mathcal{I}$ am so grateful and thankful for:

(Note what you truly appreciate. Really feel the emotion of appreciation. Utilize your five senses.)

1.

2.

3.

4.

5.

6.

7.

8.

9.

10.

Today's Priority Goals:
(Goals you must reach today.)

1. _____

2. _____

3. _____

Fun Goals:
(Goals that bring you joy.)

1. _____

2. _____

3. _____

Journal Entry/Notes:

(Use this space to expand on your thoughts.)

_____

_____

_____

_____

_____

_____

_____

_____

_____

_____

_____

_____

_____

_____

Date ___ / ___ / ___

I am so grateful and thankful for:

(Note what you truly appreciate. Really feel the emotion of appreciation. Utilize your five senses.)

1.

2.

3.

4.

5.

6.

7.

8.

9.

10.

Today's Priority Goals:
(Goals you must reach today.)

1. _____
2. _____
3. _____

Fun Goals:
(Goals that bring you joy.)

1. _____
2. _____
3. _____

Journal Entry/Notes:

(Use this space to expand on your thoughts.)

Date / /

I am so grateful and thankful for:

(Note what you truly appreciate. Really feel the emotion of appreciation. Utilize your five senses.)

1.

2.

3.

4.

5.

6.

7.

8.

9.

10.

Feeling gratitude and not expressing it is like wrapping a present and not giving it.

William Arthur Ward

Today's Priority Goals:
(Goals you must reach today.)

1. _____

2. _____

3. _____

Fun Goals:
(Goals that bring you joy.)

1. _____

2. _____

3. _____

Journal Entry/Notes:

(Use this space to expand on your thoughts.)

_____

_____

_____

_____

_____

_____

_____

_____

_____

_____

_____

_____

_____

_____

_____

Date ___/___/___

I am so grateful and thankful for:

(Note what you truly appreciate. Really feel the emotion of appreciation. Utilize your five senses.)

1.

2.

3.

4.

5.

6.

7.

8.

9.

10.

Today's Priority Goals:
(Goals you must reach today.)

1. _____
2. _____
3. _____

Fun Goals:
(Goals that bring you joy.)

1. _____
2. _____
3. _____

Journal Entry/Notes:

(Use this space to expand on your thoughts.)

Date ___ / ___ / ___

I am so grateful and thankful for:

(Note what you truly appreciate. Really feel the emotion of appreciation. Utilize your five senses.)

1.

2.

3.

4.

5.

6.

7.

8.

9.

10.

Today's Priority Goals:
(Goals you must reach today.)

1. _____

2. _____

3. _____

Fun Goals:
(Goals that bring you joy.)

1. _____

2. _____

3. _____

Journal Entry/Notes:

(Use this space to expand on your thoughts.)

_____

_____

_____

_____

_____

_____

_____

_____

_____

_____

_____

_____

_____

_____

_____

I am so grateful and thankful for:

(Note what you truly appreciate. Really feel the emotion of appreciation. Utilize your five senses.)

1.

2.

3.

4.

5.

6.

7.

8.

9.

10.

Today's Priority Goals:
(Goals you must reach today.)

1. _____

2. _____

3. _____

Fun Goals:
(Goals that bring you joy.)

1. _____

2. _____

3. _____

Journal Entry/Notes:

(Use this space to expand on your thoughts.)

_____

_____

_____

_____

_____

_____

_____

_____

_____

_____

_____

_____

_____

_____

_____

_____

I am so grateful and thankful for:

(Note what you truly appreciate. Really feel the emotion of appreciation. Utilize your five senses.)

1.

2.

3.

4.

5.

6.

7.

8.

9.

10.

Be thankful for the struggles you go through. They make you stronger, wiser, and humble. Don't let them break you. Let them make you.

Unknown

Today's Priority Goals:
(Goals you must reach today.)

1. _____

2. _____

3. _____

Fun Goals:
(Goals that bring you joy.)

1. _____

2. _____

3. _____

Journal Entry/Notes:

(Use this space to expand on your thoughts.)

Well-being tips for challenging days

1. Take a Wonder Walk. Stepping outside and being present in nature is healing. It opens the mind to experience the awe and wonder of nature.

2. Grounding. When placing bare feet on the ground, it aids the body in reducing stress. Within 4 seconds of placing feet on the ground, the body experiences physical changes and shifts the nervous system into a more relaxed state.

3. Deep breathing. Take a slow deep breath in through your nose, allowing your abdomen and chest to rise as you fill your lungs with air. Exhale slowly through your mouth. With each breath, slowly inhale for 4 seconds and slowly exhale for 4 seconds. Repeat this process two more times. This helps open the chest cavity to allow more oxygen to flood the body and signals the nervous system to calm down.

4. Reach out to a loved one via text, phone call or video chat. Loneliness leads to unhealthy living. Reaching out to a trusted friend helps confront those hard issues together. Connecting with others leads to a thriving life.

5. Create a mantra. By creating a short phrase that brings you peace and repeating that phrase will help the mind and body focus on the moment at hand. I personally use this in stressful situations or when I become nervous. It helps calm my mind knowing that I am safe. Some examples are: "I choose serenity. I choose peace." Or "I am calm. I am relaxed. I am safe."

6. Smile. The act of smiling tricks the brain into a more cheerful state. The mind releases tiny molecules to help release stress naturally.

7. Watch a comedy or funny movie and laugh your heart out. The act of laughing is similar to deep breathing. It increases oxygen in the body which helps to relax the muscles. In turn, this reduces the physical symptoms of anxiety.

These tips are supported by science and I have personally found these activities to be helpful on challenging days.